Toad to a Nightingale

DAVID R. GODINE · PUBLISHER · BOSTON

TOAD TO A NIGHTINGALE

Light Verse by Brad Leithauser

Drawings by Mark Leithauser

First published in 2007 by
DAVID R. GODINE · *Publisher*
Post Office Box 450
Jaffrey, New Hampshire 03452
www.godine.com

LIBRARY OF CONGRESS CATALOGING-IN-PUBLICATION DATA
Leithauser, Brad.
Toad to a nightingale : light verse / by Brad Leithauser ;
drawings by Mark Leithauser. — 1st ed.
p. cm.
ISBN-13: 978-1-56792-341-4
ISBN-10: 1-56792-341-0
I. Leithauser, Mark, 1950– II. Title.
PS3562.E4623T63 2007
811′.6—dc22
2007025606

First Edition
PRINTED IN CHINA

To
Bryan Leithauser
and
Mary Jo Salter Leithauser

For
Two sisters-in-law
from
Two brothers

Nightingale to a Toad

For those who are
The best, this is
The best of all
Possible worlds.

So sang the nightingale, whose song
Dropped on the toad as revelation.

I've always known
The beautiful
Are beautiful
For a reason.

So sang the nightingale, whose song
Served the toad as edification.

You'll never fly,
With neither wings
Nor song to lift
Your squatting heart.

So sang the nightingale, whose song
Struck the toad in remonstration.

And just because
You live in mud
Is no excuse
To look so soiled.

So sang the nightingale, whose song
Washed over the toad as purification.

Plant Creatures

Apple

Fruit of the tree of knowledge?
                                    Boil it down —
With sugar and a pinch of cinnamon —
You're left with an old-fashioned synonym
For nonsense: applesauce. That's all. For *this* we lost
Our digs in Paradise, yielded the crown
Of Heaven to dig a cold and moldy grave?
Bright Eve learned *nothing* — save
That education isn't worth the cost.

Muscat Grapes

The sun gives birth to cold
Galaxies of fruit, pale stellar
Clusters that warm and brighten as the weeks unfold.
Some rain, some wind, the fruit grows fat, while, high
Overhead, autumn stars restring the sky,
But still summer extends, extends, until the day
Somebody carts those lower stars away
And the sun ripens in the cellar.

Cantaloupes: "$1 Each, 3 for $2"

They're priced to sell, this stack of shabby-looking old
Moons — fissured, cratered, and a little gray,
As if they'd met some chill along the way.
They wait for someone to appear
And lift moon after moon up to his ear,
Tapping and listening. Which one — which one
Will he serve up tonight, reborn in crescents, gold
With the last glow of a departed sun?

Coconuts

Who would suppose those fronds – tough as ribs, dry as sand –
Might, as you start to doze, turn into silk
Handkerchiefs, waving hello or goodbye?
(In Paradise, comings and goings are all one.)
Your maiden voyage wakes you to a land
Of maiden aunts who giddily hoist high
Their thick mugs of warm milk
To toast the sun.

Dates

The ones who know it best are those who filed
Into the desert and got lost, tried to retreat,
Wandered for days on end, lashed themselves to
Their fading camels' necks before
Passing out – and awakened on the blinking shore
Of some small waterhole by which a date palm grew:
Dates must be heaven born. Such killing heat,
Such killing sand, could never yield so sweet a child.

Two Bosc Pears at Dawn

How many pairs of lovers could
Compare with these for harmony of form
With form, line with line, hue with hue, or show with such
Warm clarity that love's best understood
Without experience? Here's skin you needn't touch
To feel it soft and firm
At once, and flesh you needn't eat
To know it sweet.

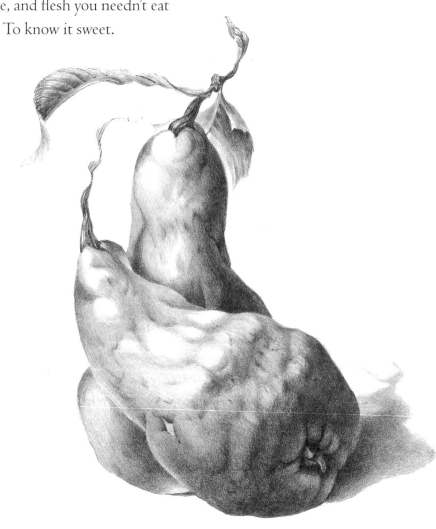

Lemons

Here's one to ripen but not mellow;
Some souls refuse to warm.
They will confer but not conform,
Adding an edge, an acid clarity
That sweetens sweetness through severity,
As we turn needfully to one
Who would go head to head against the sun
And blaze a braver yellow.

A Dropped Watermelon

The victim lies sprawled at the blazing edge
Of a vast parking lot, oozing a sea
Of red. Sharp black pellets peep through
His broken side. The sun's blinding; no one can say
Who dumped him here — a mystery
Of no never-mind to the two
Shuffling kids in T-shirts whose job it is to wedge
The body in a bag and shoulder it away.

Four from the Forest Floor

Overnight Mushrooms

The neighborhood shrines,
White as snow, show the clean hands
Of stolen labor.

A Millipede

It's the thousand legs,
Smoothing his slither, that make
Him look like a snake.

Pseudoscorpion and Carpenter Ant

Droll as a doll's dream —
This mite-sized meet, chase, close — though
The kill's genuine.

A Rhinoceros Beetle

Not dead, but dwindled,
The dinosaurs: he rears his
Snout and almost roars.

Periodic Riddles

Hydrogen

Brevity? The sole whit am I, the one
From whom if one is taken none
Remains, and if this too,
Too solid earth offers no resting place
For the *esprit* of someone who
Disdains its stony gravity, there's — outer space:
Silver skies? Gold skies? Nights and days
In turn confirm how bright the slightest soul will blaze.

Oxygen

In the dim attic's heavy stack
Of newspapers, no less than in the slight,
Bright bobbing rose of a coquette's flushed face,
I find my place,
Though years must pass, the papers turn
Yellow to brown, and brown to black,
Before the hidden headline comes to light:
BEAUTY IS BORN TO BURN.

Neon

The flashing sign
 Promising warmth (THESE GIRLS ARE HOT!),
Or novelty (NEW NUDE REVUE!),
Or elegance (SOPHISTICATED FUN!)
Or verve (LIVE GIRLS! ALL LIVE! ON VIEW!) –
Such things are mine,
 The mingled fantasies of someone not
About to mix with anyone.

Silicon

Beached up upon myself, for untold centuries
I lay inert upon the shore,
Devoid of drive and will,
Or so it seemed, though always in wait for
An inter-prising mind to seize, shape, hone
My blocky core and ultimately squeeze
Not water, no, but — rarer still —
Thought from a stone.

Gold

I have my hold
Upon your eye: you've never seen
A shine like mine — elusive-lustered, bold
And cold at once — and you shall call
Me dear forever, though the lean
Eremite on his tall
Mountain go on muttering, "All
Gold is fool's gold."

Mercury

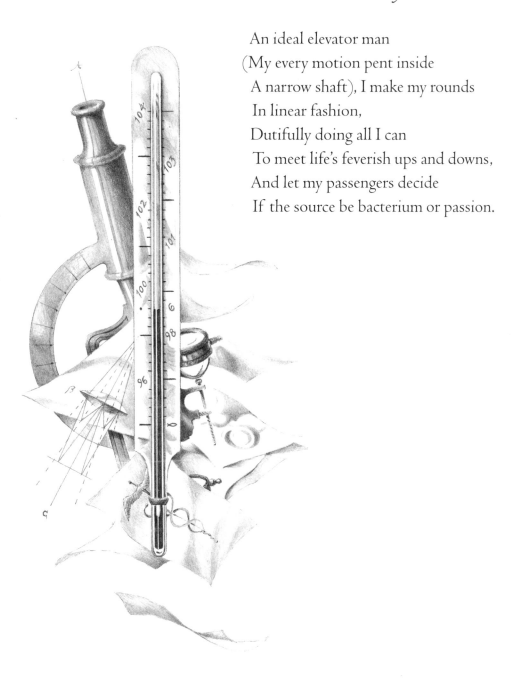

An ideal elevator man
(My every motion pent inside
A narrow shaft), I make my rounds
In linear fashion,
Dutifully doing all I can
To meet life's feverish ups and downs,
And let my passengers decide
If the source be bacterium or passion.

Lead

All roads lead to Rome, from which led
 The dark spokes of antiquity's bright plumbing,
Whose engineering ingenuity
Overlooked nothing but my tendency
 To leach in water, thereby becoming
A drink that goes right to the head
And stays there. I settle the brain.
. . . And an empire goes down the drain.

Uranium

Earth's megaflower, I unfold
A blossom far too big, too big to hold,
And in fields strewn with crystals, salts, and metals —
Lacking their knack for standing still —
I am forever breaking down. Even so,
 I've learned in passing to go slow:
The mile-high mountains will
Be milled to meal before my final petal settles.

Furnishings of the Moon

Tree

All but white in the moonlight, a stripped skeleton
Under a February moon, the tree outside
    Your bedroom window has been purified
        Gradually, losing all signs
    Of life by slow degree, except the one:
The way, when the wind's right, the bony branches bend
        To the glass, tap-tap a few lines,
            As though greeting a friend.

An Alarm Clock Powered by AAA Batteries

      Two slender bodies are the fuel
It feeds upon. You might suppose them dead
    And buried, but their hearts are beating...
    Witness the blood-bright light they shed.
It's the sheer steadiness of appetite —
Never a moment when the thing's not eating —
    That chills you in the dead of night.
    Time isn't just unjust but cruel.

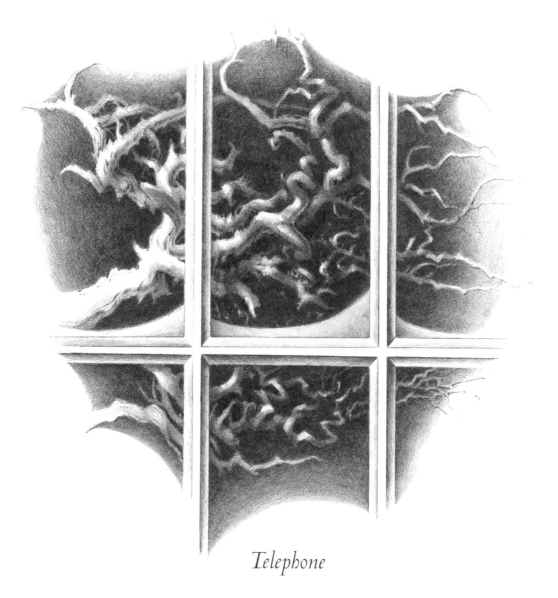

Telephone

Each night we cross a threshold where
No good can come of it: the hour's too late
For any friendly call. And if it rang?
Either a wrong number or something else — worse — wrong.
The ring's so much louder once we turn off the light. . .
And so we drift off to an unformed prayer:

Let no word come to me tonight
From anyone out there.

A Clawfooted Bathtub

A guest in an old summerhouse, you navigate
Dark hallways to a room whose antique tub is brimming
    With moonlight, find the switch – and hesitate.
They'd vanish at a touch: all those who, down the years,
Stripped and lay naked here. Everything disappears
    So easily – water to light, light dimming
To memory, memory slipping into dream. . .
Here's your wan lover, waiting in a wash of steam.

Refrigerator

A light turns on inside you like the light in *it*
    And you half-wake from your half-doze:
Its sleepy hum's the sated hum of someone who
Ate nearly *everything*. It ate the halibut,
The ham, the Jello, the ragout, the jam, the fake
Crab roll, the capers, ketchup, frozen wedding cake. . .
      And goes on humming while it grows
        Hungry for you.

Smoke Detector

There's no fire without smoke — so I'd insist
To the insomniac, for whom my bead of light,
        Dim as a cigarette
Puffed in the dark, tenders a message: *It's all right.*
    Stove's off. Furnace hasn't exploded yet.
    Lightning? Must have struck some other location.
    Mice haven't eaten the wires' insulation.
Your daughter's former boyfriend is no arsonist.

Neighbor's Radio

Maybe it comes up from below,
Or through a raised window. Anyway, there's no choice:
    You listen to your neighbor's radio...
        Or listen to his listening,
        Since you can't make out anything
Beyond the murmur of a tale whose narrow plot
Is clear: somebody else can't sleep. You're hearing not
    A voice so much as hunger for a voice.

Old Furnace

    It watches over you from down below,
        Singing the Lullaby of Warmth. They all
        Join in, none of them dead, a choir
Of parents, grandparents, grandparents' parents. . . . Small
    As a thumb, you're back in a cave once more.
    Time hasn't started yet. We do not know
We do not know. Outside the cave's mouth, predator
Howls after prey. Within, the old ones tend the fire.

Cosmogonies

Solar System

Out of the blind swamp
Nine moths emerged to circle
Our kerosene lamp.

Moon and Earth

Nights, the blanched crone drags
From her sickbed to check on
Her blooming mother.

Falling Star

Once school's out, lights out,
The old teacher scratches her
Match on the blackboard.

December Snow

By cover of night
The daily-stolen sunlight
Is returned, brushed white.

Creature Creatures

A Platypus

The egg came first.
I'd have no *point* without the round
Closed contours of that clutch cached underground.
To find one in the nest – as cool
A stone as ever hatched a lizard or a snake –
You'd think it must be a mistake
That this was something laid by someone nursed
On mother's milk. I brood exceptions to the rule.

Hooded Vultures

To see thronged vultures make a shoving sort of nest in
A creature's chest, and watch two of them quarreling
   Fiercely over a limp wet piece of string
      (A snip of wildebeest's intestine),
   Is to revisit, on a stripped-down scale,
         Something you've seen before:
   A pair of shoppers in a tug of war
Over a last-of-its-kind in a closeout sale.

Warthogs

Across the skull-strewn Serengeti Plains
On stubby legs the warthog runs. He has the air —
    Brisk, businesslike — of having just
    Recalled a meeting where he plans
To seal a deal. And leave the others in the dust.
    Were he to stop — he won't — he might declare,
    "While I don't doubt your vigor or endurance,
      You might be well served by some life insurance."

Gnu

No news of gnus is good news, it seems clear,
Since anything you're apt to hear
Will deal in shrinking habitats,
Declining populations. . .
It's a sad story, human-gnu relations.
You steal our food and homes, and that's
No way to treat a gnu — unless you'd have us be
Forever mute as our initial G.

Lemur

Caught in the act
Of stealing up a moonlit tree,
His face a mug shot in the flashbulb's glare,
Body tense, fingers blacked,
He looks out from his permanent bandit's mask,
Looks out from his progressively more bare
Shelter of greenery to ask,
Why did you take my world from me?

Water Snakes

Loosed from the lowest levels
Of dreams, we drift in in insin-
uative motions, machinating through
A milky murk, half there, half hidden. . .
We come because we always do; snakes writhed within
The Primal Sea. And as for you,
You were – before the bitter Fruit was bitten – bidden
To deal with devils.

Giant Squid

You with — so far as anybody knows —
The largest eye in all Creation
Remain unglimpsed, although our scouting vessels pass
  Through the massed blackness, hunting your habitation.
    You have glimpsed *us*, we would suppose.
    We wait to see you through the glass,
      Darkly, darkly. We know you're there.
. . . Each probe comes back like an unanswered prayer.

Fire Ants

To everyone who has been stung, we offer you
Utmost apologies, and though we might just mention
The poisons, flames, floodings we've been subjected to,
    By you, we won't. Or note that you began it. . .
          We merely ask
       There be no further intervention
While we conclude our Nature-given task:
      The conquest of the planet.

Toad to a Nightingale

No song, I fear — my broken song.
 I've nothing to offer the likes of you.
 How is it, then, I dare address
 A melodist so pure and strong
 (O melomagnipotent! Plentipotunetiary!),
From the sinking depths of my unworthiness,
 In a voice spawned in a swampy stew
 By way of the gravel quarry?

Still, I'd insist, for what it's worth,
To one whose throat the angels kissed
(Dear deliridelicitude! O opululitarose!),
Earth's fairest dreams are born of earth —
Born sometimes, even, in the scummy
Ooze of a drainage ditch . . . including those
Where I am your ventriloquist,
And you, my dear, my dummy.

ABOUT THE AUTHOR

BRAD LEITHAUSER was born in Detroit in 1953 and graduated from Harvard College and Harvard Law School. He is the author of five previous volumes of poetry — *Hundreds of Fireflies*, *Cats of the Temple*, *The Mail from Anywhere*, *The Odd Last Thing She Did*, and *Curves and Angles* — and a novel in verse, *Darlington's Fall*. He has also published five other novels and a book of essays, and edited *The Norton Book of Ghost Stories* and *No Other Book: Selected Essays of Randall Jarrell*. He is the recipient of many awards for his writing, including a Guggenheim Fellowship, an Ingram Merrill grant, and a MacArthur Fellowship. An Emily Dickinson Senior Lecturer in the Humanities at Mount Holyoke College, he lives with his wife, the poet Mary Jo Salter, in Amherst, Massachusetts.

ABOUT THE ARTIST

MARK LEITHAUSER was born in Detroit in 1950. He received a bachelor's degree in the classics and two master's degrees in the fine arts from Wayne State University, where he taught studio art. Since 1973, he has exhibited his etchings, drawings, and paintings in solo and group shows at the Coe Kerr Gallery, the Brooklyn Museum, the Corcoran Gallery of Art, the Library of Congress, the Chrysler Museum, and the Museum of American Art, and he is currently represented by the Hollis Taggart Galleries in New York City. He previously collaborated with his brother Brad by creating woodcuts for the chapbook *A Seaside Mountain* and pencil drawings for *Darlington's Fall* and *Lettered Creatures*. A senior curator and the chief of design at the National Gallery of Art, he lives with his wife, Bryan, and their two children, Hamilton and Anna, in Washington, D.C.

This book, like every book we have worked on together, carries a dedication so obvious it need hardly be expressed: to our mother, Gladys Garner Leithauser, and the memory of our father, Harold Edward Leithauser.

AUTHOR'S NOTE

Both author and artist wish to thank all the good people at the Helen Riaboff Whiteley Center in Friday Harbor, Washington, who offered us beauty and comfort in equal measure. Much of this book was completed during our too-brief stays there.

Perhaps the acquiring of emotional debts is — paradoxically — a sign of a rich life. In any event, I'd like to acknowledge a few debts, or simply to extend a few good wishes, by dedicating "Apples" to Marianne Doezema; "Muscat Grapes" to the memory of Trinkett Clark; "Dates" to Wendy Watson; "Two Bosc Pears at Dawn" to John Hennessy and Sabina Murray; "Hydrogen" to Jack Cameron; "Oxygen" to Sam and Lynn Marcellino; "Silicon" to William G. Salter; "Gold" to Philip Salter; "Telephone" to David Mohney, "Neighbor's Radio" to Carl W. Scarbrough; "Tree" to Dave Smith; "Gnu" to Sherrill Harbison. Special thanks to Nancy Novogrod, editor of *Travel and Leisure*, who offered me an assignment to Tanzania that inspired me to finish my "Creature Creatures" sequence. The title poem, "Toad to a Nightingale," sings for David R. Godine.

ARTIST'S NOTE

I would extend the lines in these drawings to connect with some special people. The rhinoceros beetle is dedicated to David R. Godine; the gnu to Carl W. Scarbrough; the dates and coconuts to Marianne Doezema and Wendy Watson; the nightingale drawings to Nick Clark and the memory of Trinkett Clark; the lantern to Katryna Carothers; the squid to Dr. Fad; the cantaloupe to Gretchen Hirschauer; the lemur to Richard Kenney; the furnace to Hollis Taggart; the apples to Molly Eppard; the pears to the pair of Carol and Doug Koelemay; the ant to the memory of Sylvia Thompson, who loved the insect world; and the bridge to Linda Kaufman, with whom I first saw the Pont du Gard.

A NOTE ON THE TYPE

TOAD TO A NIGHTINGALE has been set in Bruce Rogers's Centaur and Frederic Warde's Arrighi. Among the numerous revivals of the types of Nicolas Jenson, Centaur is arguably the most elegant interpretation of the type used by Jenson in his widely admired 1470 edition of Eusebius's *De Præparatione Evangelica*. Eager to maintain the spirit and proportions of his model, Rogers drew his letters directly on enlargements of Jenson's printed letters with a minimum of retouching. The result was a face of more distinct calligraphic emphasis with livelier letterforms than other Jenson revivals. Its bracket serifs give it an aristocratic bearing that its cousins – among them the Kelmscott Press's Golden type and the Doves Press type – lack. ∴ ∴ Commissioned as a proprietary face for the Metropolitan Museum of Art in New York, Centaur was licensed to the Monotype Corporation in 1929. Faced with the problem of creating an italic to accompany the roman – a feat he did not feel qualified to attempt – Rogers turned to Warde to fill the gap. Modeled upon a chancery italic type cut in 1527 by Ludovico degli Arrighi, the resulting type has an easy rhythm and gracious letterforms that admirably complement Rogers's roman.

Design & composition by Carl W. Scarbrough

◆　◆　◆